WHEN THE SUN FELL OUT OF THE SKY

This beautifully illustrated, therapeutic picture book tells the story of Stan the Giraffe. Stan loves the sun and to feel its warmth on his long back; but one day it suddenly and unexpectedly falls from the sky and disappears from his life. Stan experiences many different and difficult emotions throughout the story, reflecting the seven stages of grief. The story aims to normalise these feelings, which for children and those around them, can be frightening.

This storybook has been written to support key adults in helping bereaved children to find a way to cope, manage and make it through their grief.

The resource *Guide to Supporting Children through Bereavement and Loss* has been written to accompany the storybook, providing information, guidance and ideas for anyone supporting a grieving child, in school or at home.

Hollie Rankin is a counsellor who has worked with and supported children, young people and their families within schools in the North East over the last ten years. Her recent books on trauma and bereavement were prompted by a noticeable gap in resources to help to guide adults when supporting children in emotionally challenging circumstances.

For Nancy Peters MBE

Forever in our hearts

Marcus x

First published 2019
by Routledge
2 Park Square, Milton Park, Abingdon, Oxon OX14 4RN

and by Routledge
52 Vanderbilt Avenue, New York, NY 10017

Routledge is an imprint of the Taylor & Francis Group, an informa business

British Library Cataloguing-in-Publication Data
A catalogue record for this book is available from the British Library

Library of Congress Cataloging-in-Publication Data
Names: Rankin, Hollie, author.
Title: When the sun fell out of the sky : a short tale of bereavement and loss / Hollie Rankin.
Description: Abingdon, Oxon ; New York, NY : Routledge, 2019. | Summary: When the sun disappears from the sky, Stan the Giraffe goes through all of the stages of grief, then finally notices the moon and sees that he can go on.
Identifiers: LCCN 2018051792 | ISBN 9781138360440 (pbk.) | ISBN 9780429433146 (ebk)
Subjects: | CYAC: Loss (Psychology)—Fiction. | Grief—Fiction. | Sun—Fiction. | Giraffe—Fiction.
Classification: LCC PZ7.1.H3714 Whe 2019 | DDC [E]—dc23
LC record available at https://lccn.loc.gov/2018051792

ISBN: 978-1-138-36044-0 (pbk)
ISBN: 978-0-429-43314-6 (ebk)

Typeset in Calibri
by Apex CoVantage, LLC

When the Sun Fell Out of the Sky

A Short Tale of Bereavement and Loss

Hollie Rankin

Illustrated by Marcus Peters

Routledge
Taylor & Francis Group
LONDON AND NEW YORK

Stan was a giraffe.

Like all giraffes, he had long, spindly legs, and an extremely long neck.

Stan loved nothing more than to eat the greenest leaves from the tallest trees, and to feel the warm sun on his face as he crunched and munched.

One morning, Stan awoke with a start.

A strange feeling in his tummy told him that

something wasn't right.

All around him was darkness!

Stan hurried outside.

It was dark out there too.

The other animals stared up into the ink-black sky.

The sun was nowhere to be seen.

It was as if the sun had fallen out of the sky.

Stan couldn't believe what had happened.

Wouldn't believe it.

"The sun can't just fall out of the sky."

He decided it must be hiding.

He was going to find it and put it right back

where it belonged.

Off he marched.

Stan was sure it was all a big mistake.

He searched and searched and searched some more.

He hunted behind trees, under bushes, in the stream.

He stretched his neck as high as he could to see

if the sun was hiding behind the clouds.

It was nowhere to be seen.

It really was as if the sun had fallen out of the sky.

Stan felt cross.

Really angry in fact!

He clenched his teeth.

He stamped his hooves.

Stan was furious.

He spotted a grey rock on the ground. Stan kicked it with all his might into the dark sky where the sun used to sit. "Stupid sun, I hate you! You left me, and now the whole world has changed."

Stan felt guilty for being so angry with the sun.

He cried.

Big angry tears rolled off his face and down his long neck.

He knew it wasn't the sun's fault.

He felt awful for being so cross.

"I should have done something," Stan sobbed.

"I should have stopped the sun falling out of the sky."

He closed his eyes ever so tightly, and wished and prayed

for the sun to return.

He would give anything for the sun to come back.

Stan had never wanted something more in his whole life.

He was desperate to feel the sun on his face

and for the world to be light again.

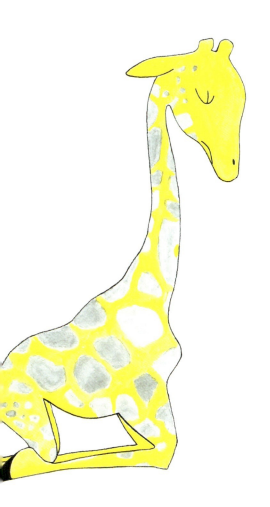

Time passed.

Stan realised that wishing wasn't working.

No matter how much he wanted to save the sun,

he knew he couldn't.

Stan felt sadder than ever before.

He felt so sad that his head ached, so sad that his legs ached.

In fact, so sad that his whole body ached, from the top of

his head, to the tips of his hooves.

It was a pain he had never felt before.

A pain that made him more tired than ever before.

Stan was exhausted.

He did the only thing he could.

Eventually, Stan lay down and slept.

The other animals were worried.

They brought Stan the greenest, juiciest leaves to eat.

Stan wasn't interested.

He wanted to be left alone, to sleep, and sleep.

And so he slept.

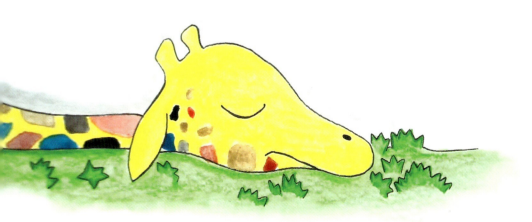

One night, some time later, Stan was woken

gently by a silver light shining above him.

Slowly, he opened his eyes.

Stan stared at the bright glow of the silver moon.

He had never noticed how beautiful the moon was before.

Stan stood up slowly.

He stretched his neck to take a closer look.

He felt the warm beams on his back.

He saw how it softly lit up the world.

Stan saw a glimmer of hope in that full moon.

He knew it could never replace the sun

that had fallen out of the sky.

The sun that he loved and missed terribly.

The world was very different now, without the sun.

But Stan thought to himself that maybe, just maybe,

there was a chance he could get used to living in this new world.

With that, Stan stood up tall, took a big, deep breath, and with the moon above him lighting the way, Stan bravely stepped onto the silver path ahead of him.

The End